HOW A SMALL INDIANA TOWN AND ITS TEAM HELPED SAVE HOOSIER HYSTERIA

H FOR HONOR

BY ALEXANDER WOLFF

PHOTOGRAPHS BY DAMIAN STROHMEYER

MASTERS PRESS

For the people
of Batesville,
for having made
this book possible

Published by MASTERS PRESS
A Division of Howard W. Sams & Company
2647 Waterfront Parkway East Drive
Indianapolis, IN 46214

This book was designed
and produced by Joe Zeff.
http://www.joezeff.com

Printed in the United States of America.

97 98 99 00 01   10 9 8 7 6 5 4 3 2 1

Library of Congress Cataloging-in-Publication Data Pending

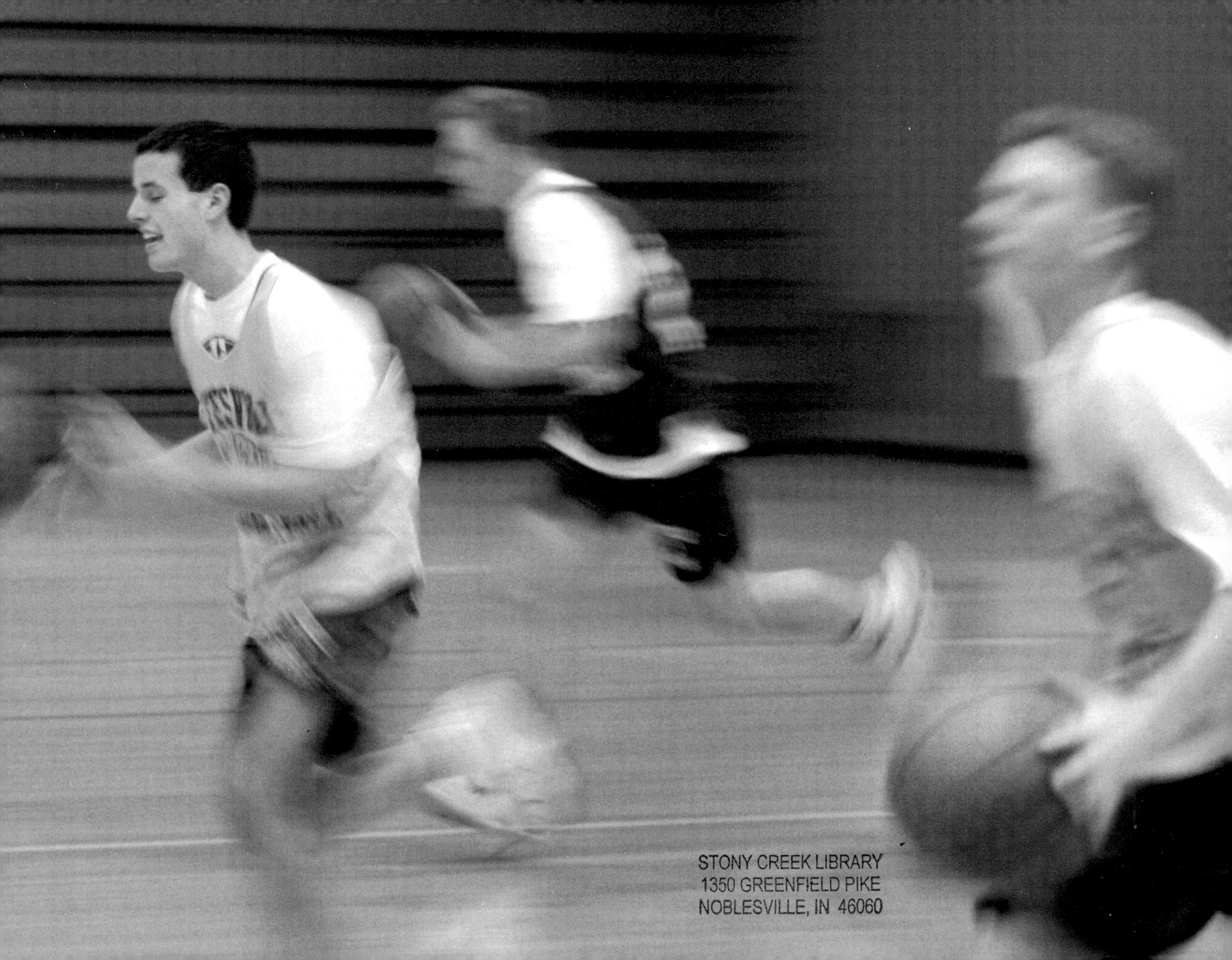

LEGACY

8

TOWN

22

TEAM

34

TOURNAMENT

50

AFTERMATH

84

ONE

LEGACY

UR STORY BEGINS WHERE IT WILL END, in a county called Ripley, believe it or not — amidst the hardwood forests and soybean fields of southeastern Indiana. Hereabouts winters are fierce but looked forward to, for that is when bandbox gyms get stoked with body heat and fevers of spirit. Besides, you can't get to spring without going through winter, and in the Hoosier State spring is that bewitching time. It's the time when basketballs, as Grantland Rice once put it, "almost hide the sky." ¶ For 87 years Indiana has proudly staged an all-comers, single-class high school basketball tournament,

begun annually in the fading days of February and finished in late March. By its end only 12 boys can call themselves state champs. The biggest school fights through the same draw as the smallest, and that helps confer on the entire event an authority that has made Indiana high school basketball famous from coast to coast.

Come tourney time, every school in the state willingly succumbs to Hoosier Hysteria, from 56-student New Harmony High in the utopian settlement of the same name, to sprawling Ben Davis High in suburban Indy, with its largest-in-the-state enrollment of 2,798; from schools with picturesque handles like Turkey Run (enrollment 164) and Rising Sun (252), to consolidated districts that go by neologisms like Tri-West Hendricks (301) and Jac-Cen-Del (228). Every spring, from Wawasee to Paoli to Loogootee, high school hoops does as much as anything to make Indiana a state of mind as well as a state in fact — something more than just West Ohio or East Illinois.

■ Milan's unlikely title is writ large there, and in the heart of every Hoosier schoolboy.

In 1954, Ripley County's tiny Milan High School, which numbered but 161

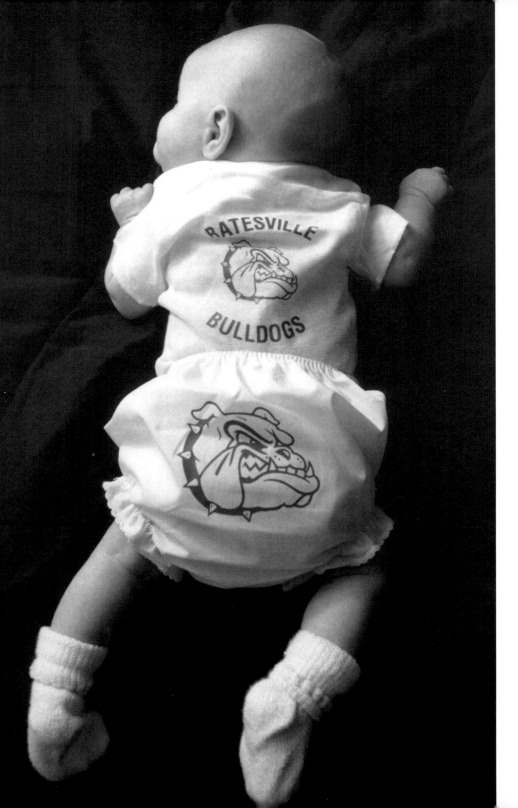

■ Olivia Brewster may one day pick up a pompon as a Batesville High cheerleader.

students, sanctified the small-town myth by winning the tournament title. That accomplishment resonated far beyond Milan itself, where some 40,000 people lined the streets for a parade honoring the victorious Indians. It has fired the imaginations of hundreds of thousands of Hoosier schoolboys in the years since. Never mind that only one school of 800 students or fewer has won the state title in the intervening 42 years, and that was fictional Hickory High in the 1986 film "Hoosiers." Down in Milan, neither the legend on the town's water tower reading 1954 STATE CHAMPS, nor the feat itself, will fade.

The prospect of the undersized gamely doing battle with the big boys has been a part of Indiana's basketball mythology since the very first game in the state's history, between YMCA teams from Crawfordsville and Lafayette in 1893. Back in the 1950s, tiny Monument City High counted only seven boys on its rolls, but that sufficed for a team of six players and a manager. For a quarter-century, the

■ Keevan Vonder-heide proudly wears the number of his big brother, Bulldog guard J.D.

Bloomington *Herald-Times* has honored this tradition by choosing a "SmAll-State Team" entirely from schools serving the state's hamlets and backwaters.

But in April of 1996 comes apostasy. The Indiana High School Athletic Association board votes to experiment with multiple state tournaments, one for each of four enrollment classifications, for at least two years. A majority of the state's high school principals ratifies the change a short time later, and it seems inevitable: No longer will latter-day Milans be able to dream of challenging the Ben Davises and Fort Wayne Northrops and Gary Westsides in the postseason. No longer will schools big and small, most within a short drive of one another, meet for local bragging rights in the tournament's 64 score-settling sectionals. No longer will a school have to win two games a day on three straight Saturdays to become state champs. No longer will the plug of a big-city high-rise and the socket of a downstate limestone quarry connect and electrify the state for four weeks each spring. No longer will every schoolboy player in Indiana be shooting at the same goal.

■ **The view from Jim Menser's easy chair: son Michael going against guard Brad Sandifer.**

The change is supposed to spread happiness by spreading more postseason hardware. It it supposed to force the big boys to pick on someone their own size, and give the little ones a better chance to shine. Yet according to the IHSAA's own polling, a clear majority of the state's players oppose the move to class basketball. Those who elaborate on their opposition unfailingly cite tradition, but they also invoke the chance, the fight, the dream — all that the Miracle of Milan stands for.

So as the 1996-97 season gets under way, Indiana is left with a case of go-figure: The adults in charge want standards lowered, and the kids want the bar left right where it is; educators are saying winning is important enough to rewrite the rules, and players and students are saying, No, there are more important things — the taking part, the gallant try.

EXIT 156 OFF INTERSTATE 74 — IT'S RIGHT NEAR THE billboard for Indian Lakes RV Resort ("Call 1-800-42SEEYA") — will take you to Milan. But continue north another 15 miles or so, not yet crossing the county line, and you'll come upon the town of Batesville. The two towns share more than just Ripley County and a passion for basketball. Batesville High principal Fred Sagester spent nine years teaching in Milan, and his wife still does. Before Mark Ferguson took over as BHS athletic director, the job belonged to Glenn Butte, who had been a sophomore on Milan's '54 state champs. Mel Siefert, Batesville's 34-year-old coach, occasionally plays golf with Butte, who has screened for him a tape of the final, in which the Indians put away mighty Muncie Central 32-30. And when Michael Menser, Batesville High's senior star, drives to Aurora to visit a friend, he always stops for a sundae at the Milan Dairy Queen.

Up in Broad Ripple, the yuppified neighborhood north of Indianapolis, the proprietor of Plump's Last Shot has his own interest in the Batesville Bulldogs. Bobby Plump is the 5'10" guard who sent a soft jump shot splashing into the net to win that championship for Milan High, and he thinks the IHSAA is out of its gourd. Plump runs a lobbying group, Friends of Hoosier Hysteria, and he counts as allies in his fight against class basketball such Indiana icons as Steve

■ **No practice begins without defensive slides, a regimen reflected in the team's statistics.**

Alford, Damon Bailey, George McGinnis and John Wooden. "Certain coaches and principals want a so-called 'state championship' on their resumes, and that's the overriding reason for the change," he says. "The IHSAA board and the high school principals say they're doing it for the kids. But the kids don't want it.

"They're doing the kids a great disservice. Tell them again and again that they can't compete, and pretty soon they'll start believing it. There were 751 teams in the tournament the year we won. 750 didn't win it. Were they failures? Certainly not."

Besides calling for a nonbinding referendum on the issue and lobbying the legislature to intervene, Plump and other anticlass activists have taken testimony. They point out that after Daleville (enrollment 258) defeated Anderson (1,502) for a sectional title in 1985, Broncos coach Everett Gates said the victory meant more to him than a class state title he had won years earlier in Ohio. They point out that after Randolph Southern (240) whupped Richmond (1,919) in the sectional in 1994 (Randolph's first victory over

the Red Devils in 40 years, drawing a five-mile caravan to the regional), Rebels coach Dave Wall said that the win thrilled him no less than a state class title would have. They point out that Ted Kitchel, the All-America whose Indiana University team won the NCAA crown in 1981, considers the sectional championship his Cass High Kings won in '78 just as sweet. And they point out that Wooden counts the state title he won as a Martinsville Artesian in 1927 as more meaningful than any of his 11 NCAA crowns.

Further, the Plumpites provide evidence that the little guys can too compete. They point out that Turkey Run beat Center Grove High, a sub-urban Indianapolis school more than nine times larger, for the 1996 title in girls' softball, which is one of six other sports scheduled to join basketball in a class system. They gesture south at Kentucky, which with Delaware and Hawaii would be the lone holdouts playing an all-comers tournament: In '96, little Paintsville High, with 229 students, won that state's boys' title, beating a succession of bigger schools along the way. They cite Minnesota's storied state ice

■ **Cheerleaders Jill Hardebeck, left, and Kristin Lucas pledge allegiance to the Bulldogs.**

hockey tournament, where the average crowd is way down since multiple classes began in 1992.

Why, back in '94, when their current seniors were fresh-men, the Batesville Bulldogs themselves had reached the semi-state against Ben Davis, and gotten their teeth into the Giants' legs, gnawing away at 38-all midway through the third quarter. The city kids ultimately pulled away. But Batesville knew it mighta, coulda, maybe even shoulda.

Plump will spend the season monitoring the for-tunes of tiny Union (Dugger), a school with 134 stu-dents that had gotten notice in the press as a possi-ble Milan in this last year of single-class basketball. When tournament time comes around, he'll be invit-ed down to Barr-Reeve (enrollment 176) to fire up the Vikings. But Plump would just as soon see Batesville outfitted with a slingshot. "I've followed them all year," he says. "Batesville over-all has the best talent of all the small schools in the state."

Every Batesville Bulldog can recount minutiae from the Miracle of Milan: How the Indians fielded a team from but 73 boys; how on their way to the title they beat Oscar Robertson's mighty Indianapolis Crispus Attucks team; how Snapshot McGee, a character from Indy, camped out in town for three weeks, printing up photos to meet the demand; how Plump had learned to shoot in a hayloft. Just in case, each of the past two seasons before the regionals, Siefert gathered the team at his house to watch "Hoosiers," which is based on the Milan story.

"If they took a vote of the people in the state, it wouldn't even be close," Siefert says. "My gut says they're going to have to go back."

With an enrollment of 589 through four grades, Batesville would be among the smallest schools in the 3A classification, the second largest of four groupings planned for the 1997-98 season. To a man the Bulldogs sneer at the proposed change; in spirit each sounds more Milanese than breaded veal. "'State titles,' plural, doesn't sound good to me," says Aaron Ertel, one of Batesville's seniors. "Class basketball takes away from the honor and glory of what a state title should be about. I like to say, 'Even if we don't have any class, we'll always have our dignity.'"

"I'd rather lose a game like this to a team like this than win

■ At each workout, every boy practices dozens of free throws to prepare for game situations.

some other state title against somebody else," Menser, the Bulldogs' star, had said after New Castle (enrollment 1,157) eliminated Batesville a year earlier on a shot at the buzzer.

Going into the 1996-97 season Menser is a Plump-sized 5'10" and 145 pounds, a senior who would love to play for Indiana. He'll sign instead with Indiana State, because Hoosiers coach Bob Knight believes him to be a couple of inches too short to play in the Big Ten. It's hard for Menser not to note the similarity between how he is regarded and how his team is. "People have told me I'm too small to play Division I ball," he says. "Well, I don't want to be categorized as small. And our team doesn't want to be categorized as small, either.

"I like to think we're carrying the banner for all the small schools out there," he adds. "It would be a great honor if we could do what Milan did — to be the Milan of the '90s."

To carry a banner; to be a modern Milan. Those are the twin causes that Batesville's Bulldogs are playing for. Their season will be a processional, always with chins up, to and through the tournament in March. Theirs will be a march for honor.

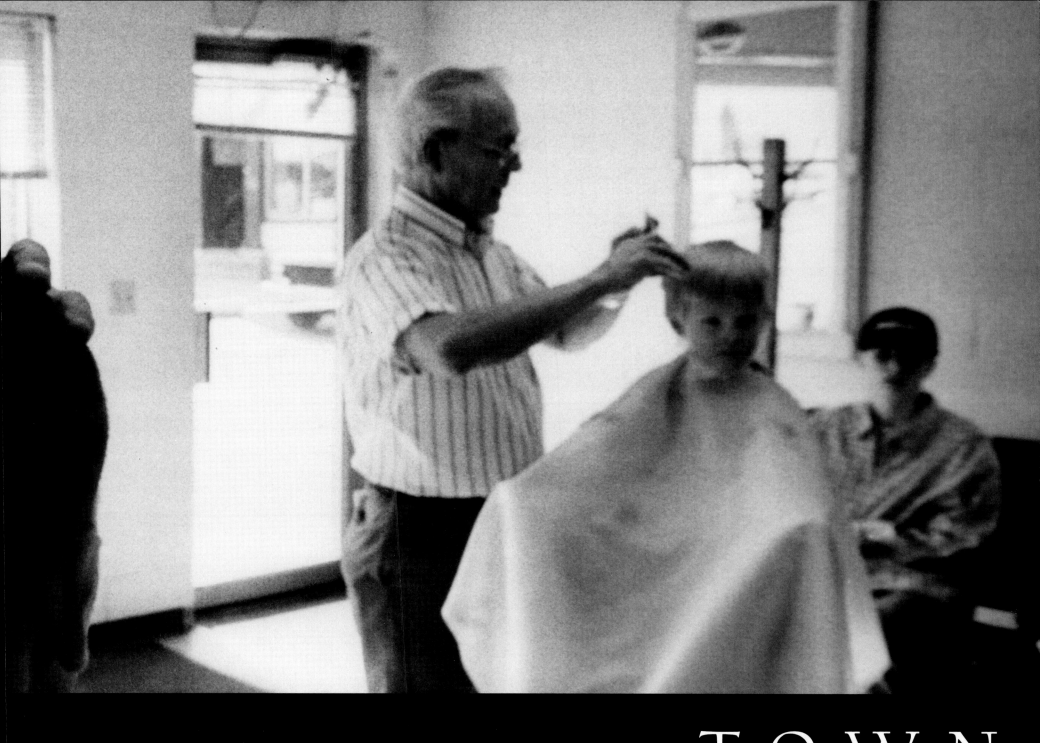

TOWN

ATESVILLE IS SMALL, BUT NOT SO SMALL that it doesn't have sports talk. Some patter can even be found on the radio, on *Chalk Talk*, the weekly show on WRBI. But the most trustworthy verbiage comes unplugged: over morning coffee at Fran Telles' barber shop on the town square; with a lunchtime cup of homemade mock turtle soup at the Hobo Hut out Highway 46; as a side dish with a fried chicken dinner at Feltz's Family Restaurant downtown. ¶ The talk is hopeful, supportive, knowing. It's always seasoned with sober Hoosier skepticism and the occasional healthy second-guess. "I

jumper, of course.

Thursdays at 6:10 p.m., about 10 minutes after Fran has dropped the blinds, locked up and begun sweeping the tailings from the floor, Michael Menser will knock three times. "He knows it's me," Menser says. Fran lets him slip in and gives him a trim, and Michael brings along a pie — always large pepperoni — from the Pizza Haus next door. "It started out as something fun to do," says Menser. "Now we don't want to stop doing it."

Batesville (pop. 5,000) sits just off Interstate 74, some 45 minutes northwest of Cincinnati and about an hour southeast of Indianapolis. Legend has it that the German immigrants arriving in the 19th century were drawn by the thick forests that reminded them of the *Schwarzwald* many had left behind. Stands of oak, walnut, ash and cherry made for sturdy furniture, railroad ties, church statuary and caskets. The paneling in the chambers of the statehouse up in Indy is Batesville-cut, too.

wish they'd all meet in one place," Mel Siefert says of these Greek choristers. "Then I could make just one stop."

If he had time to stop but once, Siefert would alight at Fran's. There the men caucus over their coffee and hammer out a consensus, which this season holds that the Bulldogs have their best chance in memory of winning the regional. God willing, the creek don't rise, and Aaron Ertel buries the open

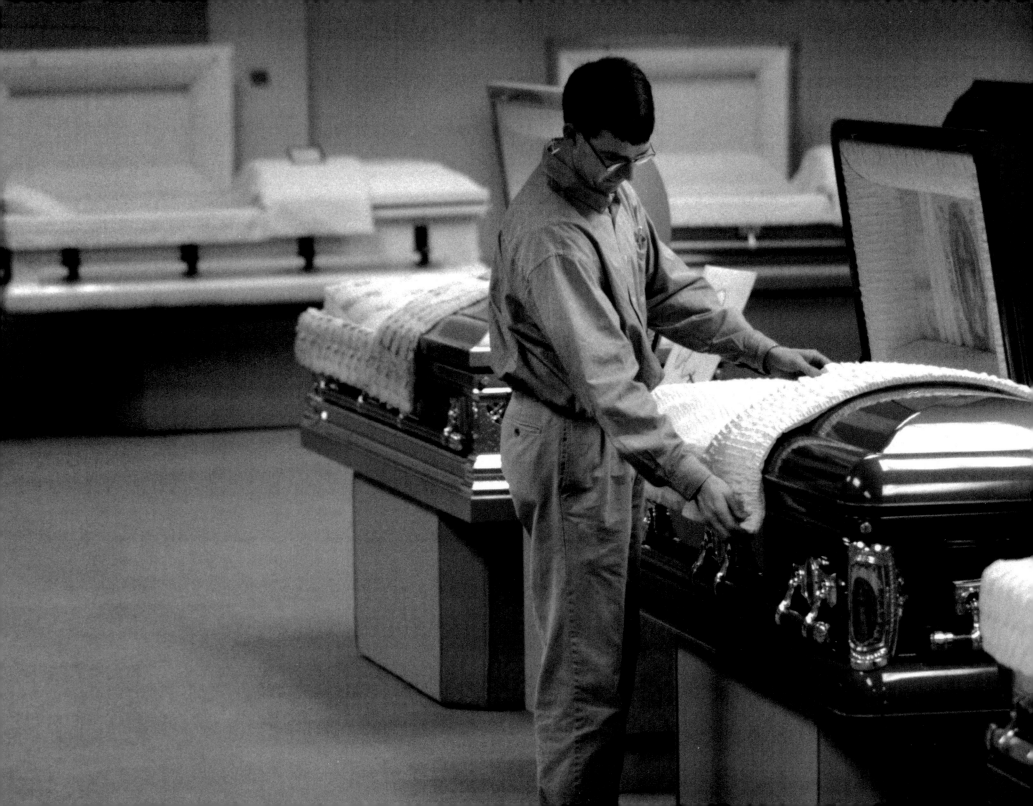

The downtown storefronts evoke the citizens' Teutonic forebears. The Pizza Haus and Feltz's are just the start of it. The names of businesses in town — Lindemann Appliances, Romweber Furniture, Schmidt's Bakery, Nolte's Pharmacy, Fullenkamp Sporting Goods, Weberding's Carving Shop, Koch's Auto and Truck Repair, Pulskamp's Carpet — are echoed by the roster of the Batesville High boys' varsity, with its Bohman and Ertel, its Gartenman and Menser, its Obermeyer, Vonderheide and Wagner.

Today General Electric warehouses nine million light bulbs on the outskirts of town. Batesville Tool and Die casts auto parts. And more than a dozen Delta pilots, assigned to the airline's hub at Cincinnati International, call Batesville home. But the town is more than anything identified with Hillenbrand Industries, the $1.6 billion Fortune 500 company that employs 3,700 people in its hospital furniture, burial insurance and Batesville Casket divisions. Trucks from the latter make deliveries to funeral homes all over the country, with the admonitory lettering across

■ **Top-of-the-line caskets grace the showroom floor at Batesville Casket Co.**

the back — PLEASE DRIVE SAFELY; HEAVEN CAN WAIT — usually drawing smiles from motorists who see it. Small wonder that, upon telling fellow Hoosiers where they're from, Batesvillians often hear in return, "Oh, the deadest place in the state!"

Get beyond the morbid associations, however, and Batesville is a place marked by indomitability. It's a place where a G.E. executive, in town for the first time, asked a Chamber of Commerce host, "Did you call up everybody and ask them to mow the grass?"

It's a place so shot-through with boosterist spirit that its slogan — "You can't beat Batesville!" — works for the Chamber of Commerce and the high school cheerleaders alike.

It's a place where the St. John's United Church of Christ (Huntersville) has sponsored a family of Bosnian refugees (although the heedless basketball style of the Brnjaks' hoop-crazy boy, Goran, makes him unsuitable for the BHS varsity).

It's a place where kids amuse themselves with the simplest

■ Like so many Indiana communities, Batesville began with a town square and grew outward.

YOU CAN'T BEAT "Batesville"

■ The same article of faith works for both Bulldogs fans and the Chamber of Commerce. things, like going out to the airstrip to watch the Hillenbrand jets take off.

It's a place where people look disapprovingly at East Central High, the largest school in the conference, because of its emphasis on football. "There, basketball is just something to do in the winter," says Ertel, who went to East Central until his sophomore year. "It's like . . . an *Ohio* high school."

It's a place where over the years the basketball has usually been good, sometimes been great, but always been prized. Two-thirds of the town can squeeze into the high school gym, and Batesville fans travel well: More than 1,000 will make the trip up to Kokomo for a game this season, and when the Bulldogs take to the road, Mark Ferguson says, "We may end up beating 'em by 40 points, but their A.D.'s grinning ear-to-ear."

It's a place where a senior on the one Batesville High team to reach the Final Four of the state tournament, Jim Fritsch, went on to become mayor. Whatever else may have been on Fritsch's resume, every

■ Esther and Harold Prakel of Western Avenue are loyal Bulldogs boosters.

citizen knew that, having been a member of the 1943 Bulldogs, he had what it takes.

■ Former Bulldogs coach Paul Ehrman catches up with Siefert at the Hobo Hut.

It's a place where superintendent Jim Freeland, talking contract following the board's decision to hire Siefert, shot the new coach a wink and said, "Maybe I should pay you by the victory."

And it's a place where a page in the program distributed at Bulldogs games features the following stanzas:

Please don't curse that boy down there; he is my son, you see:
He's only just a boy you know, he means the world to me.

I did not raise my son, dear fan, for you to call him names:
He may not be a superstar, and these are high school games.

So, please don't curse those boys down there, each one's his parents' son,
And win or lose or tie, you see, to us, they're number one!

Indeed, you can't beat a place that's rich in both light bulbs and caskets and — as the Bulldogs will prove — every shade of human emotion in between.

TEAM

I T ISN'T HARD TO FIELD A TEAM IF YOU'RE A high school basketball coach in Indiana. Mel Siefert knows there will be three aspirants for every place on the Batesville roster. So he begins the weeding-out process over the summer, in the predawn hours of days in June and July, when dewdrops and crickets scarcely hint at the remorseless heat to come. ¶ Boys roll out of bed by 5:30 a.m., knowing that the gym at the high school will be unlocked by 6. These aren't — can't be — official tryouts, but two hours of weightlifting and scrimmaging, five days a week, do as much as anything to make clear who will be a Bulldog and who will not.

■ **Senior Brad Sandifer is a tricaptain and a sweet-shooting swingman.**

"Some kids," Siefert says, "aren't willing to pay that price."

There will be no slackers or dodgy characters on the team that's ultimately chosen in the fall. There will be good students, including several on the honor roll; there will be boys who organize a charity three-on-three tournament over the summer; there will be young men who get involved in the Readers Are Leaders program over at the intermediate school (read 15 books, get a free ticket to a Bulldogs game); there will be teammates who together spend a day over every Christmas break volunteering in a Cincinnati soup kitchen.

Paul Coulis is the father of Christian Coulis, a senior frontcourt reserve. He's also an executive with Hill-Rom, Hillenbrand's hospital furniture division, and a guy some think deserves a hospital ward of his own: He'll show up at games in a blue-and-white wig, and turn cartwheels on the sidelines, and once jawboned all the dads into painting their faces. As any number of parents might have, he went to Siefert after a game in which Christian didn't get any minutes. But

■ **Siefert is sometimes pressed into duty as the team's video scout and launderer.**

here is what a summer's careful winnowing, and the team spirit it creates, can do: Papa Coulis didn't want to know why his son hadn't played; he simply wanted to know what he ought to tell Christian to keep him positive and focused on the good of the whole.

Batesville won its first sectional title back in 1927, and the Bulldogs have added 13 since, including an unprecedented three in the past three years. Even more cherished are the school's six regional titles — in 1934, '43, '51, '52, '71 and '94 — and of course that '43 appearance in the Final Four. As heir to all this history, Siefert would seem to deserve royal status. But the school district can't let him while away his time dreaming up new inbounds plays. So he spends six hours a day teaching government. Over the summer he moonlights as manager of the community pool. Before ascending to head coach of varsity basketball he paid his hoop dues for six seasons, first as a varsity assistant, then as freshman coach.

Siefert grew up in Oldenburg, the German settlement a few miles outside Batesville, a Catholic enclave commanded by

■ Siefert's son, Ben, is a regular at practice, whether horsing around with Menser ...

the spires of its churches and convent. He had been a pretty good forward in his day at Batesville High, but an even better quarterback, and it was in that role that he hooked up with his wife, Amy, a cheerleader, in a pairing he admits is "pretty cliched." A dogeared copy of John Wooden's *They Call Me Coach* graces his office, and a spool of thread sits on the ledge of the bulletin board above his desk — evidence of one of the many hats he wears, that of tailor if some player should rip his uniform. Indeed, if Batesville has back-to-back, Friday-Saturday games, Siefert will go into his office at 5:30 on Saturday morning, to do laundry and watch film.

Siefert and his six seniors were thrown together in 1993, and he has grown with and groomed them over a quadrennial. Batesville won the New Castle regional in Siefert's rookie season, going 20-4 before losing to Ben Davis. Finishes of 17-6 and 23-2 followed. As they embark on their senior season, members of the class of '97 are the first Bulldogs with an opportunity to win four conference

■ ... or walking in his father's shadow, ready to take charge at a moment's notice.

titles and four sectionals in a row.

"They know the game," the coach says of his seniors. "They love the game. With them you don't really need to teach. You just need to remind."

So whiskered are Siefert's Bulldogs that they have three captains. One is Michael Menser. Though he's as slight as anyone on the team, Menser won the Ironman award during summer workouts for pumping more than four times his body weight in three different lifts. Joining him are 6'5" forward Aaron Ertel, the wraithlike jump shooter whose accuracy is a bellwether for the team's offensive fortunes, and 6'2" swingman Brad Sandifer, Menser's best bud, the hoop junkie whose ingenuous manner leads teammates to call him Mr. Obvious.

The other senior starter, Justin Wagner, is a 5'10" guard whose defensive crouch would make a summer-camp station-drillmaster swoon. Matt Maple, a fearless 6'3" junior whose father, Dave, played on the Batesville varsity in 1971 and '72, starts too, holding down the middle.

Siefert can look down his bench to

■ **Not 20 years ago, Siefert was the kid on the floor. Now the players hang on his every word.**

Clint Bohman, the junior shooter who seems to get more confidence with every minute he plays; Gabe Westerfeld and Scott Gartenman, the junior backups up front; and Jeremy Day, Patrick Kaminski, J.D. Vonderheide and Michael Williams, their counterparts in the backcourt. Coulis and Nick Obermeyer are off-the-bench post defenders and rebounders. Meanwhile Ben Siefert, Mel and Amy's 10-year-old son, is equal parts mascot, manager, oral historian and assistant coach.

But wherever the Bulldogs are going, it is Menser who will take them there. Whether the moment calls for a pass, a shot, or a clever bit of dribbling, he has a knack for providing. He shoots (52% from the field, even as two of every five shots come from beyond the three-point arc); he scores (25 a game). At the line he is cash money (87%). The ball is so safe in his dexterous hands that he makes twice as many assists as he commits turnovers, even as he attracts the outsized attention of defenses. Only Maple, the team's center, grabs more rebounds, and then only by a few.

Given the position he plays, his

■ **When working a practice drill, two passing Bulldogs always share some skin.**

45

command of fundamentals, his devotion to the game, and his rank and citizenship in school (he finished the year ninth of 123 overall, with a 96 average, and was involved with student council), Menser would seem to be central casting's candidate for Mr. Basketball, the statewide award virtually every Hoosier schoolboy dreams of winning. There's even legend to gild the Menser story: His mother Jenny, a primary-school teacher, has a key to the gym, and beginning when he was a third-grader she let little Michael shoot while she graded papers.

Alas, the honor of Mr. Basketball will almost surely go to someone from a bigger school. Jenny and her husband, Jim, who works as safety director at the tool-and-die factory, have asked that Batesville High not campaign on their son's behalf, fearing that the politicking will detract from the rightful priority of the team. But if the Bulldogs were to pull a Milan, Menser would attract huge support. As it is, he's a cinch to win Mini Mr. Basketball, the award for players 5'10" and under.

Menser had gone out to a huge tournament in Las Vegas the previous sum-

■ **In sync, both on and off the court: Brad Sandifer, Justin Wagner and Matt Maple.**

mer, with an AAU team based in Bloomington, and there he had stood out so starkly from the hundreds of others that he made the 12-man all-tournament team. Yet apparently the big-time coaches can't justify finding a place for him. Their blindness scarcely eclipses the view of Bobbie Brandes, the secretary in the school's main office. Menser is "Batesville's best ever," says Brandes, and she, being BHS class of '48, would know.

Menser is at his best as the Bulldogs open their season, at South Dearborn just before Thanksgiving. Batesville appears beaten with one second to play, but Knights coach Rob Moorhead runs out onto the floor in premature celebration, and the ensuing technical sends Menser to the line. His two free throws provide Batesville with a 69-68 victory and an auspicious if heart-stopping start. An 87-61 defeat of Milan — blessed Milan — in the Ripley County Tournament in mid-December leaves the Bulldogs 6-0. At the Hall of Fame Classic

■ No huddle gets broken without the players chanting, in unison, "Team!"

in New Castle after Christmas, the Bulldogs score their biggest victories yet, knocking the socks off the Madison-Grant Argylls, and then defeating mighty, sixth-in-the-state Anderson to take the title. (When the Argylls beat DeKalb — which is two-and-a-half times their school's size — in the consolation game, hopes of all would-be Davids are given a further boost.)

Not until early January, after nine straight victories, is Batesville's record sullied. The Bulldogs travel to Kokomo, where they hold a nearly game-long lead — it's 10 with three minutes remaining — before the Wildkats prevail on a put-back basket with three seconds to play.

Since that night in January the Bulldogs haven't lost. Not even the challenging stretch that ends their regular season — six of eight games are on the road — can flummox them. They're 22-1 and No. 3 in the rankings as Hysteria is about to set in. But throughout the state hundreds of other teams, and thousands of other boys, are also cocking for one last shot. They all harbor the same desire as the Bulldogs, and most play for teams that are bigger and deeper.

That scarcely troubles the boys from Batesville. "Others might have better athletes," says Ertel. "But we have a better team."

FOUR

TOURNAMENT

IF BATESVILLE IS A SLEEPY TOWN, SLUMBER BRINGS vivid dreams come tournament time. In late February the high school turns into a hothouse of sign-painting and pep-rallying. The men begin lining up outside the barber shop at 7 a.m., even though Fran doesn't open 'til 8. Every storefront in town shows its spirit in its own way. "Furnish us with a victory!" urges a furniture store. "Bulldog Basketball is contagious!" warns a pharmacy, while a bank proclaims, "We're banking on a Bulldog victory." ❡ The sectional over

in Greensburg awaits, and it seems as if the only adult male in town not to go by the barber shop is Mel Siefert. "I can't," the coach says. "It's at the point now where it's hard even to go to Kroger. I know people mean well. But I don't have the time."

The sectional serves to winnow the 382 teams to a contending 64. But it is also the state tournament in microcosm. Small schools are thrown in among big, with geography the common denominator. One must be a "from here," not a "come here," to fully fathom the passions felt by schools all within a half-hour's drive of one another.

Tuesday night's opener in Greensburg helps illustrate the instant redemption possible in a sectional. If Batesville is a long shot of statewide renown, the Chargers of tiny North Decatur, winners of only two games all season, are the local Davids. Using a spread offense, North Decatur leads Greensburg, the largest school in the sectional, virtually the entire game before suffering a 54-53 loss. One of the Chargers' most passionate fans, Patty Reding, will tell Batesville's *Herald-Tribune* that the outcome, heartbreak-

■ **In the high school art room, the cheerleaders hope to chalk up some team spirit.**

Four starters relieve tournament tension with an on-the-road game of euchre.

ing though it is, does nothing to weaken her opposition to the changes the panjandrums of the IHSAA have in store. "If anyone could make a case for class basketball, our school should be able to," she says. "But this team just had one of the most exciting evenings of their season. In traditional Indiana basketball, tourney time means you throw out the records, and you bring your emotion. That's what this team brought with them for their final game.

"So what if a Milan never appears again? The dream is really more than who will win the state championship. The dream is beating your biggest rivals, maybe even only once every five or 10 years. And an upset in a local sectional will be remembered by the entire community."

Batesville is a relative Muncie Central to its first opponent, South Decatur. The Bulldogs score the game's first 13 points and lead 22-6 after the first quarter. In the end, 11 players score in Batesville's 60-33 victory.

Next up is Jac-Cen-Del, representing the cobbled-together district to Batesville's south. As affluent as

Batesville is, Jac-Cen-Del is rural and proud of it. The week leading up to Thursday night's game is capped by "Drive Your Tractor to School Day." (At Batesville, cracks Menser, "We would have a 'Drive Your Cherokee to School Day.'") There is nothing the Eagles would like more than to beat "the preps."

Batesville knows that its opponent isn't accustomed to losing, and the Bulldogs play accordingly. Menser sprints after a loose ball in the first quarter, turning his ankle as he stumbles over a newspaper photographer and out of bounds.

Menser's absence helps Jac-Cen-Del take a 15-7 lead. Though Menser only sits out for several minutes, and he will go on to score 27 points, Batesville is up by a mere 34-33 at the half. The Bulldogs ratchet up their defense in the third quarter, forcing seven turnovers in that period alone. But Jac-Cen-Del is as ready as North Decatur to test its sectional rival. Down 11 with six minutes to play, the Eagles string together eight straight points, and in the game's dying moments they have a chance to tie or win. That's when Jac-Cen-Del's Basil Dean, trying to gather in a lead

■ For big games, a caravan of Bulldogs fans falls in faithfully behind the team bus.

■ Both mascot **Matt Prentice** and the **Bulldogs** — with motivational material posted on each player's locker — go through pregame rituals.

■ **Come the sectionals, proper preparation entails limbering up both physically and psychologically.**

pass with five, four, three seconds to play, takes his eye momentarily off the ball. It runs off his hip and out of bounds.

The 71-69 loss ends the Eagles' season at 18-3. All three of those losses came to Batesville. Tonight, they have shot 65% in defeat. For the school's 228 students, a dozen of whom had been on the business end of a 70-48 Bulldogs victory in January, there is pride and disappointment in equal measure. "If they'd beaten us," Mark Ferguson says, "it would have been as important to them as a state championship would be to us."

Batesville's opponent in Friday's sectional final is Greensburg, the sectional's hosts. Aaron Ertel and Matt Maple run into foul trouble, but Clint Bohman makes good use of his extra playing time, scoring nine points. Meanwhile Menser is continuing his season-long mastery of the Pirates. He will score 33 points, 21 of them on seven majestic threes. "One man show!" the Greensburg students chant, but their words are nothing more than a quibble. Once again the Bulldogs are reliably served by their third-quarter D, which limits the Pirates to a single basket.

■ Here, Siefert says, "I'm not screaming at 'em, I'm screaming to 'em."

■ With school pride on the line, the shirts come off and the war paint goes on.

With its 64-54 win Batesville is now one of 64 sectional winners to advance to 16 regional sites. After the game, all Batesvillians reconvene back at the high school, filling the bleachers in the gym to hear the six seniors and coach Siefert voice their gratitude, and receive the town's thanks in return.

On Monday, mayor Bill Abplanalp, gracing his proclamation with three "whereases" and one "now, therefore," certifies what hardly needs to be made official. In Batesville, Ind., it is Batesville Bulldog Week.

FOR THE FOURTH TIME IN FOUR YEARS, SIEFERT AND his seniors are making the trip north to New Castle. If they can beat Connersville on Saturday afternoon in New Castle's huge Chrysler Field House, the Bulldogs will yet again face the bigger, deeper Trojans on their home floor.

The seniors' last two visits to New Castle ended with defeats in the final seconds. This time, however, Batesville

■ Menser cruised against Greensburg, as he had twice during the regular season.

■ Batesville played the role of scrawny crasher against its larger host, Greensburg.

has more wins than any team in the history of the school. And so powerful is the Milan mystique, and so pervasive is the backlash to the IHSAA decision to tinker with Hoosier Hysteria, that even the hardened members of the media, polled before the start of the tournament, pick Batesville to win it all. "I think it's more a sentimental thing," says Ferguson. "The press would like to see a smaller school have success. Hopefully that won't jinx us."

The Bulldogs know that the press' prognostication is driven more by sentiment than reason. But they also know this: If they hadn't blown that 10-point lead at Kokomo in January, they would be unbeaten and ranked No. 1 in the state.

One year ago Batesville had felt the sting of losing the regional semifinal to New Castle, when the Trojans' off-balance, wrong-handed, 35-foot three-point heave banked home at the horn. (At the horn or after the horn? Ask BHS principal Fred Sagester, and he pauses a beat, then says, "As an administrator, I have to

■ Tourney spirit, courtesy of Holly Denninger, Tessa Appleton and Brandi Nobbe.

say 'at the horn.'") In 1995 the Bulldogs had lost to Connersville by two. But in 1994, when these seniors were freshmen, they had survived two Connersville shots in the final four seconds and beaten the Spartans for the regional crown.

On Wednesday, as they have before the regional every year, the players' fathers join the team for the bus ride up to New Castle for an evening practice. Afterward they all stop for dinner. Tucking into T-bones at Ponderosa, dads and lads alike know what has already been decided down at the barber shop: that these Bulldogs have as good a chance as any Batesville team ever to advance to one of the four semistates, whose victors, in turn, compose the Final Four in Indianapolis. Dave Maple, Matt's dad, is nonetheless impressed by what they have already accomplished. "The kids don't realize what a big deal it is to get this far," says Maple, who in 1971 played on the Batesville team that reached the semistate. "Now I realize what a huge deal it was. It's still a big part of my life, 25 years later."

Meanwhile, Batesville is in a frenzy. The school's original ticket allotment of 1,411 is long gone, and Ferguson is busy try-

ing to wheedle a few more seats out of the folks at New Castle. (Eventually he'll score another several hundred tickets.) The cheerleaders have their own entreaty: "Show that Bulldog Pride is City Wide!" In response citizens are tying blue-and-white ribbons to their mailboxes. They're planting yard signs by their driveways. In 1971 Menser's uncle Tom Buck had lost to New Castle and its huge center, future Indiana All-America and NBA star Kent Benson, in overtime in the semistate. "Next year it might be easier to make the semistate of a class tournament," says Menser. "But that's not even close to what we'd feel like if we were to win on Saturday."

In response to another plea from the cheerleaders — "Boost the Bulldogs on their Tourney Journey!" — more than 100 vehicles will muster in the parking lot behind the school on Saturday morning for a traditional Hoosier caravan.

Headlights on and police escort in tow, the caravan pulls out at precisely 9:15, falling in smartly behind the team bus. This is no grim cortege bearing the casket of the traditional all-comers tournament. The cars

■ Menser stands tall as he tries to block a Trojan's shot during the regional final.

■ Gabe Westerfeld and Christian Coulis come off the bench in more ways than one. are turned out in loud blue-and-white war paint. Gaudy Klaxons sound as the caravan rolls up Highway 3, past fields softened by hard rain. The caravan slows as it passes through Rushville and past Rush Memorial Hospital, where J.D. Vonderheide's grandmother, Barbara Howard, has stuck a yard sign out front: J.D. WAS BORN HERE.

Finally the bus docks at New Castle, where to Siefert the routine is familiar by now. The coach has grown fond of the janitor who welcomes the Bulldogs with what seems to be sincerity; he has come to enjoy slaking his thirst with lukewarm water at that same Freon-poor cooler outside the same locker room.

Superstition has already interceded: Siefert didn't invite the team over for another screening of "Hoosiers," the film that served as a prelude to losses in the last two regionals. But he had hoped to replicate one circumstance from '94 by requesting a lucky bus driver — the same guy, as it happens, who had chauffeured the team to the Hall of Fame Classic here back in December. Alas, a different driver has shown up.

As the tension builds, Siefert makes sure the Bulldogs have their signals straight.

■ A high school coach knows that sheer preparation can only take a team so far.

Siefert hardly has to remind his team of what happened a year ago. But before his team takes the floor for its 12:30 p.m. semifinal against Connersville, he does so anyway. "I still ache from last year," he says.

This is not the time, however, to explicitly bring up what has lurked in every exhortation he has uttered all season. "We play for Batesville first," Siefert will explain. "And if it happens to help the cause of single-class basketball, that's fine. But if I start talking about that now, that's too much pressure."

Connersville is coached by Howard Renner, who played for Bob Knight at West Point. But the 11-11 Spartans are weakened by a drinking incident that has sidelined one of their best players. Ertel has his stroke. He bottoms out two first-half three-pointers, and Batesville's 57-39 victory comes easily.

After the game there is encouraging word from Indy: Ben Davis is gone from the tournament, bounced out by a much smaller school, Indianapolis Cathedral.

High school principals, terrified at

■ B.J. Gartenman, a wrestler, might as well be a basketball Bulldog, too.

New Castle celebrates its 61-58 victory over Batesville and the regional title.

what might take place if their students were left overnight in some distant town, have long insisted that the entirety of the regionals, as with the semistates and Final Four, be squeezed into a single day. So at 2 p.m. the Bulldogs make the mile ride to the Best Western Raintree just south of town, to rest up until their 8 p.m. rematch with New Castle, which was an easy 56-37 victor over Winchester in the other regional semifinal.

As the Batesville bus pulls out into traffic, a cry issues from the back. "Hey! Someone flipped us off!"

"They're just letting you know you're No. 1," Siefert says.

HE IS NOW A LAWYER IN INDY, BUT ROBERT HAMMERLE is Batesville-born and raised. He calls his father, also named Robert, back in Batesville just after dinner. The elder Hammerle is 77 and not as spry as he once was. But son knows father well enough to place him in the kitchen on this night, stalking around, listening to the radio.

"You ready for the battle, old man?"

"What battle? Is there something going on that I should know about?"

"Don't mess with me, Pappy. You got your seat belt on tight?"

"You know, son, I really think we can do it this year. This town really believes. But it's important to remember that it's just a game!"

The two exchange nervous laughter, a "Go Bulldogs," and hang up.

THE CAPACITY OF NEW CASTLE'S CHRYSLER FIELD House, 9,325, makes it the largest high school gym in the world. Every citizen of Batesville could be accommodated nearly two times over. It seems as if at least a quarter of the town has shown up when the Bulldogs return that evening for the regional final.

"They say success is where opportunity meets preparation," Siefert tells his players in the locker room. "You've prepared for this all year. This is why you worked out at 6 a.m. over the summer. It's an opportunity nobody at Batesville has ever had, to beat the No. 1 team in the state."

A barbershop chorus croons the national anthem, then "Back Home Again in Indiana." And the game is joined.

The *Greensburg Daily News* has called Batesville's defense "stickier than the floor of a movie theatre," and against New Castle it is Milk-Dud magnificent. So is Menser, whose NBA-distance three-pointer at the end of the first quarter gives the Bulldogs a 16-8 lead. The lead stretches out to 20-10 — it's an advantage Menser will later describe as "scary, almost" — and 23-17 at the half.

But the Trojans can stand taller and go farther. In the second half they stick a chaser on Menser. Batesville has no one who can look New Castle's big guys, 6'8" Joey Gaw and 6'7" John Bryant, in the eye. Justin Wagner picks up his third foul with 11 minutes to play, by which time the Trojans have strung together several three-pointers and moved narrowly in front. Brandon Miller, Menser's opposite in the New Castle backcourt, is slippery with the ball, and though Menser is getting the better of the matchup, Batesville is tiring noticeably. With 1:42 to play and New Castle up 46-45, Menser drives into the lane and draws

■ There is a certain stillness as players absorb the pain of another loss to New Castle.

■ **One needn't have played to feel inconsolable after three such endings in four years.**

a foul, only to pull up with a cramp.

In Indiana in March, there's drama in every charley horse. Two years earlier Indianapolis Cathedral might have won a state title if three players hadn't cramped up in overtime of the team's regional final against eventual champion Ben Davis. Under the IHSAA's proposed format, regionals will entail only one game per day because of the smaller number of schools in each class draw. So one could say that the IHSAA is jeopardizing yet another tradition, a tradition that has been as much a part of the tournament as buzzer beaters and sectional upsets — the tradition of Saturday-night cramps.

Perhaps it's the cramp that causes Menser to sink only one of two free throws. Then again, the cramp may be no hindrance at all. Moments later, with five seconds to play, Menser forces overtime by dropping in two more free throws, and in the extra four-minute OT he'll add a three-pointer and a couple more foul shots.

But the Bulldogs have no one capable of challenging Gaw.

In the final half-minute, New Castle's massive center converts a Miller miss into a put-back. Then, following Menser's commission of his fifth foul, Gaw sinks two free throws. Then he steps in to deflect Wagner's desperate attempt to find Maple in the lane as the final seconds tick down. New Castle has won, 61-58.

Menser finishes with 22 points. He is the finest player on the floor. Given a slightly larger gene pool from which to draw, he and his teammates would surely be ticketed to the semistate up in Indy the following week. Thus it occurs to someone to ask, as someone had asked a year earlier, whether a school like New Castle shouldn't pick on someone its own size. Whether there might be something to this class basketball business.

Menser gives the query some thought. "Right now it hurts real bad," he says. "It's the second year this has happened. But do you think class basketball could match the atmosphere here tonight? I guarantee you, when I look back at it, I'll rather have gone out right here, this way.

"This is what it's all about. And they're killing it."

AFTERMATH

"SO HERE WE ARE AGAIN." ¶ MEL SIEFERT'S VOICE wheezes through the silence of the Batesville locker room. There is something timeless about this moment, and not merely because Batesville has once again lost at New Castle in a regional. Time, rather, seems suspended. Still-developing adolescent bodies are hunched and motionless. Siefert and his assistants, Jeff Evans and Dave Wolferst, have that grave and private cast that adults rarely let kids see. Tears seem intent on taking their bittersweet time evaporating. ¶ "You guys played your hearts out," Siefert is saying.

■ Menser, a runner-up for Indiana's Mr. Basketball title, will suit up for the Sycamores of Indiana State.

"You did everything you needed to do to win. Several times you could have died, and you didn't. Nothing will ever take away from what you've accomplished.

"Seniors, I thank you for four great years. I don't think I could have gotten any more out of you than what you gave. You played your hearts out this year, every night out.

"Now you've got to turn the page. Move on to different things. New careers, new goals.

"You younger guys, get ready for next year."

THE NEXT MORNING, ROBERT HAMMERLE, who still rues being eliminated from the sectional as a Bulldog in the '60's, will compose this letter to the editor of the Batesville *Herald-Tribune*:

"It's Sunday, March 9, and to paraphrase the Tin Man in 'The Wizard of Oz,' I know I have a heart because it's breaking. I'm from Batesville, you see, and we lost in overtime to New Castle last night.

"This school of 500 from a town of 5,000 flirted with greatness. This team, led by Michael Menser, the baddest

■ As a 3A school, Batesville will regroup next season with junior-guards-to-be Williams, left, and Kaminski.

Bulldog of this extraordinary group, was as good as anyone in the state. They gave no quarter and asked for none. They only needed fate to smile on them. But fate is cruel, particularly when a small school always has to play the big boys on their home court.

"Cinderella died. Once again, the slipper didn't fit. The big, ugly stepsister got the prince and his new castle. Or maybe I should say that New Castle got the prince.

"But let there be no mistake. The Batesville boys died with their boots on. Like the legendary 300 Spartans, they were carried home on their shields. The whole town had its heart ripped out, but it could not have been more proud. Every now and then defeat is ennobling, and so it was in New Castle last night.

"At least now I understand why I root for the Buffalo Bills, Greg Norman and Native Americans in old western movies. I see why I find Atticus Finch's defense of an innocent black man named Tom Robinson so inspiring in *To Kill a Mockingbird*. They all failed to achieve the one thing they sought, to the exclusion of all else. But, in the process, they gave us a glimpse into the soul of the human condition. Maybe the victor gets the spoils, but they proved how to find victory in defeat. So did my hometown."

Hammerle goes on to cite these words of Teddy Roosevelt: "The credit belongs to the man who is actually in the arena, who strives valiantly, who knows the great enthusiasms, the great devotions, and spends himself in a worthy cause … and who, at the worst, if he fails, at least fails while daring greatly, so that his place shall never be with those cold and timid souls who know neither victory nor defeat."

Yet even as Hammerle composed his letter, a wondrous thing was happening. Somehow the great enthusiasms and great devotions of the people had coalesced into a swollen, insistent, persuasive chorus of voices. The players and coaches and fans vested in Hoosier Hysteria, the Michael Mensers and Mel Sieferts and Robert Hammerles alike, had found the ears of their elected representatives. A bill was being readied in the state legislature that would replace the

■ **Win or lose, the people of Batesville will always take pride in the efforts of their Bulldogs basketball team.**

IHSAA with a new organization to govern high school sports, a board of seven people to be elected by the public at large. The pols up in Indy had counted heads — counted them inside the solemn chambers lined with paneling crafted of Ripley County hardwood — and the votes were there to push the measure through.

To forestall its own demise, as much as to give the people what they wanted, on April 9 the IHSAA hastily distributed a memo to all the principals and athletic directors in the state. In an 11-0 vote, the board had decided that class basketball would go forward for at least two years, as scheduled, and that there would indeed be four separate class champions. But to placate the legislature there would also be a Tournament of Champions, tacked on at the end of March, for the four class titlists. And only the winner of *that* would be crowned Indiana state champs.

The compromise didn't entirely preserve Hoosier Hysteria as Indianans had come to know and love it. The sectionals would still lose their neighborhood feel, and no longer

would March feature those Saturday-night wars of attrition, marked by cramps of the mind and the body alike. But every schoolboy in the state would still be dreaming the same dream. And in two years, when the entire ill-conceived experiment would come up for evaluation, Bobby Plump and all the other friends of what had served the state so well for so long would be able to make their case anew. Steve Witty, coach of Ben Davis and no fan of the compromise, raised the obvious question. "If we're going back to having one champion," he wondered, "then why did we go away from the original tournament anyway?"

BATESVILLE PROVED TO BE RESOURCEFUL in coming to terms with its grief. The morning after the New Castle game, at Mel and Amy Siefert's church, the Rev. David Johnston built his sermon around the Bulldogs' valor. Menser would be stronger for the experience. Before heading off to Indiana State, he toured with the Indiana All-Stars; when the All-Stars made an exhibition stop at the Batesville High gym, Little League games had to be rescheduled so the town's worshipful young could be on hand. (In

■ **Having marched as far as they could during the 1996-97 season, the Bulldogs found the aftertaste to be bittersweet.**

June, not 48 hours after Menser had lost nine pounds because of a stomach virus, the pride of Batesville went for 17 points, seven assists, five rebounds and three steals in a 102-88 Indiana All-Stars victory over their Kentucky counterparts.) Siefert, too, bounced back. He was chosen as an assistant coach with those same Hoosier All-Stars, and even got a look-see for a vacant assistant's job on Knight's staff in Bloomington.

"What a way to go," said Ertel. "To have all the small schools in the state backing you, supporting you.

"You know what I'm totally against?" he added. "I'm totally against conformity. You go into an employment office, the first question you'll get is, 'What do you have that others don't?' What separated Indiana all these years was our one-class system. We shouldn't be thinking, 'All those other states have class basketball. Why don't we?' When you have a good thing, you should stick with it."

Menser said, "The whole year the goal we set wasn't only for ourselves, but for all the other small schools out there. It would have been a great honor if we could have done what Milan did. If we could have been the Milan of the '90s."

In the end, that they hadn't didn't really matter. They had made much the same statement in their own way. They had said that you can't sell glory inflation to kids — that in Indiana, in the 90's, kids want an honest shot at a title in 1954 dollars.

There is a quote from Cervantes, a favorite of John Wooden's, that gets just right what the people of Batesville knew, and eventually the decision-makers up in Indy may fully come to understand. "The journey," it goes, "is better than the end."

THE SAME DAY ROBERT HAMMERLE COMPOSED HIS letter, he called down to Batesville once more, in search of consolation. He asked his father to please repeat for him what he had said the night before, just before tipoff — that business about this all being just a game.

Pappy Hammerle started to do so once again. Then he cut himself off.

"Dammit, Bobby, it's so much more!"

THE END